Blue and Gray
Roses of Intrigue

Rebecca D. Larson

 THOMAS PUBLICATIONS
Gettysburg **PA 17325**

Contents

Introduction

Throughout the annals of time, men have gone into battle while women have remained in the background as caregivers and keepers of the homefront. The Civil War was, perhaps, the first major conflict where women broke through the once-masculine ranks of secret agents to serve their country in a manner quite unexpected.

The chivalrous attitudes so apparent during this era provided an opportune backdrop for female operatives carrying messages to Union and Confederate generals. In an ironic twist, these strong-willed and dedicated women took advantage of their femininity and perceived vulnerability on their dangerous, often life-threatening missions.

The small band of adventuresome ladies proved that they were capable of serving their country in a manner far different from the standard roles of women in that time. Female operatives developed ingenious methods for securing information on the position of enemy regiments and records of elaborate plots. With incriminating evidence on their persons, spies crossed battle lines and infiltrated social circles to deliver messages that had the power to alter the course of the war. And while sometimes recognized by their superiors, the sacrifices made by these women have been historically undervalued.

When the tales of the Civil War are told and legends and myths are unfolded, most of the stories revolve around generals, famous battles and the contributions of male leaders. It is a rare occasion when the female agents who advanced the fame of these leaders are mentioned, and even more rare when they are acknowledged in their own right. This book is an attempt to rectify this injustice and honor these brave women who devoted their lives to their respective causes.

Rose Greenhow

During the Civil War, a small but adventuresome band of women on both sides chose not to follow the standard paths of women in war. Instead of serving as wash women, cooks, nurses, and ladies-of-the-night, this strong-hearted group was drawn into a ring of espionage and deception. Although many of these ladies were widely publicized by the newspapers, balladeers, and legend-seekers, historical evidence corroborates much truth in the renditions of their exploits. These women boldly and bravely served their respective causes at great risk to their lives. They deserve their place in the annals of history—they are worthy of honor.

Among the most notable of the Confederate lady spies was Mrs. Rose O'Neal Greenhow (1815-1864). As the widow of an influential statesman, Robert Greenhow, Rose was exposed to the aristocracy of Washington, DC. Her social position gave her access to many officials in high places, and her beauty made her the center of social attention. Blessed with olive skin, long black hair, and dark eyes, Rose Greenhow's sharp wit and dynamic manner soon won her the nickname "Wild Rose." [1]

When the war broke out, Rose did not profess Union loyalty. Although she resided in Washington, DC, she did not conceal her sympathies for the Confederacy, and her candid personality was considered one of her many charms by her admirers on both sides. Even her friends in President Lincoln's government, such as Secretary of State Seward, continued to visit her home.

The thought of betraying the confidence of her friends never entered Rose's mind until May 1861. As the Civil War began, a friend, Captain Thomas Jordan, stopped in to bid Rose farewell. Captain Jordan had resigned his commission in the United States Army and was leaving to join General Beauregard's Confederate troopers. Rose expressed a desire to contribute to the cause but felt helpless. Jordan and Mrs. Greenhow then conspired to select and recruit other members for an espionage ring. Although the entire roster will never be known, the ring included Colonel Michael Thompson, a Washington based South Carolinian code-named "Colonel Empty"; William T. Smithson, a local banker; Dr. Aaron Van Camp, Rose's dentist; a spinster housewife, Bettie Hassler; Lily Mackall, Rose's devoted friend; and Betty Duvall, the youngest of the group at age fourteen. [2]

On one occasion, Rose sent Betty Duvall, dressed as a country lass and driving a farm cart, to carry a message to Beauregard's brigadiers. After spending the night with Confederate sympathizers at China Bridge, Virginia, Betty donned a stylish riding habit and continued to the Fairfax, Virginia Court House where she was stopped by Confederate pickets. Upon locating General M. L. Bonham, Betty entered the security of his office, reached up and, according to General Bonham, "took out her tucking comb and let fall the longest and most beautiful roll of hair that I have ever seen. Calmly, she then took from the back of her head, where it had been safely tied, a small package, not larger than a silver dollar, sewed up in silk." [3]

In the packet was a ciphered note informing the Confederates that "McDowell has certainly been ordered to advance on the sixteenth R.O.G."[4] The deciphered message was rushed to President Jefferson Davis.

The ciphered message had been prepared by Rose using a special code that she and Captain Jordan had devised before his departure. Rose worked feverishly to gather every tidbit of information possible and forward it to the Confederate Army, including any pertinent information revealed by her Washington friends. Most of the messages were hidden inside the women's undergarments. One of her earliest messages to General Beauregard reached him on July 10, 1861, which informed him that the Federals would be advancing through Fairfax and Centerville. This was the beginning of a long communication line between Rose Greenhow and the Southern generals. Years after the decision by Rose to become a spy, she wrote "To this end, I employed every capacity with which God endowed me, and the result was far more successful than my hopes could have flattered me to believe."[5]

Maryland-born Rose Greenhow moved in the best circles in Washington. High-ranking Northern military officers paused for admittance to her drawing room on Sixteenth Street, as did congressmen, diplomats, and businessmen. Her flattering attentiveness caught every significant word while her analytical brain retained all the information. Furthermore, despite the most stringent counter-espionage measures the North could establish against her such as putting her under constant surveillance, Rose Greenhow repeatedly succeeded in passing vital information to the Southern officers.

One of Rose's favorite haunts was the Old Capitol Prison where she and other patriotic Southern ladies in Washington took food and clothing to the Confederate soldiers imprisoned there. After several visits, however, Mrs. Greenhow was forbidden entrance by the War Department for passing notes believed to be war secrets. Following this action, it was obvious that she was under suspicion. Rose Greenhow was not to be deterred, however. She kept her social calendar and boasted openly of her knowledge pertaining to cabinet decisions and war fortifications. She was under constant surveillance by government detectives, and to those who discouraged her

Rose Greenhow with her daughter, "Little Rose," at the Old Capitol Prison.

activities, she flatly replied, "The devil is no match for a clever woman."[6]

Fearing she or her residence might be searched, Rose made certain that nothing incriminating could be found. She hid her private papers in her library behind the books on the top row, and her secret code was kept in a secret compartment in her camisole at all times.[7]

About a month after the first Battle of Bull Run, Rose, upon returning home from a social engagement, found several men waiting for her. She was placed under house arrest and the War Department agents ransacked her home for evidence, which they never found. Rose asked what the charges were when she was placed under arrest, and she was told, "communicating with the enemy in the South." Rose smiled and replied,

> If this were an established fact, you could not be surprised at it. I am after all, a Southern woman. And I thank God that no drop of Yankee blood ever polluted my veins...all whom I have ever honored or respected have been driven by ruthless despotism to seek shelter in the South, it would seem the most natural thing that I should communicate with them.[8]

The complete records of Rose's spy organization were still in her library. This was an unthinkable breach of elementary security precautions but Rose was an amateur spy, operating without the benefit of past experience. Fortunately for Mrs. Greenhow, the Union counter-intelligence was equally inexperienced. While under house arrest, Rose bribed the Union detectives guarding her with brandy and then crept into the library to burn all the incriminating evidence. She tucked her final message to the Confederates into her stocking because the act of searching a lady in the 19th century was not proper conduct. This message was later sent with Bettie Hassler to General Beauregard.

After the deception of her guards was revealed, Rose was not allowed a moment of privacy; even while she slept a guard was stationed at her open door. Rose chafed from the strict surveillance. But, despite the best efforts of Union intelligence and their detectives, Rose-in-custody proved to be almost as dangerous as Rose-on-the-loose and even more of an embarrassment. Incredibly enough, she continued to function as a government agent, and Colonel Jordan, according to the Confederate records, continued to receive dispatches from Mrs. Greenhow for months after her arrest.[9] The Government was unable to separate Rose from her best courier, Lily Mackall, until the beginning of 1862.

The arrangement at Rose's house soon changed as other Southern ladies were imprisoned in the Greenhow home. The detectives were replaced by a detachment of soldiers commanded by a handsome lieutenant named Sheldon, whom Rose found sympathetic and courteous. While the other women were not allowed to communicate, Rose managed to charm and bribe her captors into delivering innocent-looking trinkets to certain friends, who in turn, sent them on to Southern officers. She also sent numerous letters of protest to Washington officials with regard to her incarceration, comparing herself to Marie Antoinette. To prove to her captors that they could not stop her messages, she sent a copy of one of her Washington letters to a Richmond, Virginia newspaper. The letter was printed, much to the embarrassment of the soldiers, and this resulted in the women being moved to the Old Capitol Prison.[10]

Rose's cell was a small second floor room overlooking the prison yard; her captors hoped it would discourage her communications with the outside world. The cell was poorly furnished and Rose complained bitterly until furniture and items of convenience were brought from her home. The prison superintendent attempted to make her comfortable but she had no intentions of being comfortable or content.

Two main desires burned in Rose's heart. First, she hoped the Confederacy would capture Washington, and therefore, set her free, and second, she dreamed of a public trial for which she continually rehearsed. Those in high government offices who had given her information, unsuspectingly or otherwise, trembled at the thought of Mrs. Greenhow's trial. She was prepared to defy the entire government, and while in prison awaiting trial, she took pleasure in causing chaos. Once she used her sewing machine to make a Confederate flag which she hung from her window, and on another occasion, she loosened the floor boards of her cell and shared fresh fruit with the Southern prisoners below her. Furthermore, she refused to allow the prison doctor to treat her when she was ill, and forced the authorities to call a doctor of her choice.

After three months of imprisonment, the government was ready to hear Mrs. Greenhow's case. But to Rose's dismay, the trial was held before an appointed commissioners' council, and not the public, as she had planned. Her hopes were further darkened because she was forced to wait in the anteroom for a full hour before her trial. When she was finally taken into the courtroom where Judge Pierrepont and General Dix, an old friend, were

The Old Capitol Prison at Washington, D.C.

conducting the hearings, she was treated with every consideration. They questioned her about the charges that had been placed against her, and instead of answering, she demanded to know what proof the government had against her. The judge replied that there was evidence that she sent messages to the Confederates prior to Bull Run, but she replied that she was "not aware of having done so, for [she] was not in a position to get [that] kind of information. But if [she] had secured such material, it would have been [her] sacred duty to send it to [her] friends." [11]

When asked if she would like to return to the South, Rose startled the commissioners by replying that she definitely would not. When asked if she would remain in Washington and take an oath of allegiance promising not to aid the enemy, Rose retorted, "You should blush to ask me to do that." [12]

General Dix questioned Rose about her secret code found among her clothing and the papers found in her library stove that had not burned. She admitted to creating the code out of boredom but denied its use; the judge insisted and stated: "But you did send the enemy information." And Rose simply stated that the information, if she had, must have come from President Lincoln's friends, who should be held responsible, as well. In spite of intense questioning, Rose refused to implicate her informers, and the hearing was terminated; Rose was returned to her cell to await the decision.

Two or three days after the trial, a rumor came to her that she may be sent to Boston Prison. Rose could not endure the thought of Boston, and she immediately wrote to the commissioners stating that she would be happy to go to Virginia. A few days later, she was told to prepare to leave at once, and she was then escorted through the prison hall to bid the other prisoners farewell. Apprehensive once out of the prison, she carefully questioned the captain of the guard, and only after she was assured that she was not going to Boston but to Baltimore, did she step into the waiting carriage.

Rose reached Richmond, Virginia on June 4, 1862. Later that same day she was visited by President Jefferson Davis, as well as many other Confederate officers. During these visits her friends encouraged her to travel to England to solicit funds from British sympathizers and encourage English manufacturers to buy Southern cotton. She was a great success, and everything she did gained British support for the Southern cause. [13]

In the fall of 1864, Rose returned to America via a blockade runner. The steamer ran aground on a sand bar on the North Carolina coast on September 30. Fearing Union capture, she and two other agents asked to be put ashore. A boat was lowered, and shortly after the three agents entered it the heavy surf capsized the boat. The two men were saved but Rose had her waist belt filled with golden sovereigns and the weight pulled her down. Her body washed ashore on October 1, 1864, [14] and in gratitude for her services to the Armies of the South, she was buried in Wilmington, North Carolina with full military honors.

Antonio Ford

Another well-known Confederate agent was Antonio Ford (1838-1871) of Fairfax Court House, Virginia. Antonio was twenty-four years old when she played a spy in a placid, yet lethal, manner. Her soft, dark hair was parted in the center and drawn loosely to the back of her head; she had dark eyes surrounded by long heavy lashes, a slightly tilted nose, and full lips which made her a figure of smiling prettiness.[15] Her dreamy behavior yielded a unique style to her espionage because she talked of everything except the military affairs of which she actually wanted details.

Her father, a Fairfax storekeeper, opened his home to Union officers in order to gain information, as well as to supplement his income, and Antonio made good use of the situation. She regularly transmitted information to General J. E. B. Stuart.

Early in the war, a Yankee officer ordered a thorough search of all the houses in Fairfax. Miss Ford was forewarned and had gathered her important papers and documents and hid them. When the soldiers arrived at the Ford house, Antonio sat reading in her parlor with her skirts spread wide around her chair. She calmly told the men to search all they wished, and all the while she sat reading her book. At the end of the search, the officer in charge asked Antonio to stand. Her dark eyes flashed in fury, and she said, "I thought not even a Yankee would expect a Southern woman to rise for him!"[16] and the abashed officer left in haste while the papers remained safely hidden under her skirts.

Just before the Second Battle of Manassas in August 1862, Antonio acquired information that she knew General Stuart must receive. She could get no one else to carry the message, so she hitched a team of horses to her carriage and started on the twenty mile trek. Rain slowed her journey, and she dodged many prowling Union troopers in an attempt to reach Stuart's camp in time. J. E. B. Stuart was so impressed with her performance that he commissioned her his honorary aide-de-camp. The commission forced all of Southern heart to obey, respect, and admire Antonio Ford all the days of her life.[17]

Antonio's reputation grew as her escapades were publicized by Southern and Northern newspapers alike. The Union spy-buster, Lafe Baker was determined to stop her, but before he could set a trap, she helped snare Federal General Edwin H. Stoughton.

John Singleton Mosby.

Edwin H. Stoughton.

Stoughton, commander of the Second Vermont Brigade, made his headquarters in the Ford residence and his troops were bivouacked about five miles away. Stoughton planned a gala affair at his headquarters complete with champagne and caviar, and meanwhile, twenty miles away, Confederate General John Mosby was planning his own party with Antonio as his hostess.

The Yankee festival began early in the day, and food and liquor flowed like milk and honey in the land of Canaan. The mood and the dancing were light, and Antonio quickly became the "belle of the ball." During this time Mosby surrounded the red brick Ford house and as the guests and sentries left the party or made themselves accessible, they were captured by the Confederates without a shot being fired. Telegraph wires were cut to avoid any communications, and Mosby's party was almost complete, except for the guest of honor.

The Union general, intoxicated with liquor and the festivities, went to his room to sleep off the effects. Mosby sent a man to knock on the general's door shouting "Fifth New York Cavalry; bearing dispatches for the general." When the door opened, a hand clapped over the mouth of a drowsy guard, the other hand pinned him to the floor. The big general was snoring deeply, still clutching a champagne bottle, when Mosby pulled back the quilt and slapped him on the backside. The general awoke with a snort and jumped up.

"Did you ever hear of Mosby?" the Rebel officer asked.

"Yes!" Stoughton, answered quickly, obviously thinking he was looking at one of his own men, "you've caught him?"

"He's caught you." Mosby replied.[18]

The South was ecstatic, the North dumbfounded. How Mosby accomplished such a feat was unbelievable. Stoughton's reputation was ruined but Lincoln was not sorry for him. He was more disappointed at the loss of the 60 horses that Mosby captured along with the general. The event motivated Lincoln to place Antonio at the top of Lafe Baker's list. A female detective was dispatched to Fairfax to trap her, posing as a Confederate lady from New Orleans who had taken refuge in Fairfax. The spy, whose name was Frankie Abel, arrived at Rudolph Ford's home wearing a faded old calico dress. Her tale of woe at the hands of Yankee soldiers outraged Fairfax citizens and her act was so convincing that she won the villagers, as well as Antonio's, confidence. Frankie was petted and pampered just like one of the Ford family; her shabby clothes were replaced with Antonio's stylish ones and her tears of sorrow were even dried from her deceitful eyes with Antonio's own lace kerchiefs.

Frankie stayed in the Ford home for two months, all the while working on the case. During this period, the two girls exchanged feminine confidences before retiring to bed on several occasions. The New Orleans Yankee boasted of her work for the Confederacy, and Antonio lifted her head proudly and told her how she and Mosby had captured Stoughton. She even showed the stranger her prize commission from J.E.B. Stuart.

In a few days, the "Confederate from New Orleans" said her good-byes and soon thereafter Federal agents arrived at the Ford home. Finding herself caught unprepared, Antonio could only watch in horror as her home was scoured for evidence. The Federals uncovered a large amount of information including Antonio's commission, and much to her chagrin, the Washington newspapers reproduced it as a horrendous document.[19]

Antonio was arrested and escorted to Carroll Prison (where the Library of Congress now stands) by Major Joseph C. Williard who, ironically, had escorted her to several Fairfax parties in an earlier, happier time. However, Antonio was not the only one arrested during the Fairfax raid; ten others, including her father, were jailed. Even though Mosby denied her assistance, Antonio was tried and convicted on charges of treason and jailed in the old Carroll Prison for several months.

Finally, late in September 1863, after suffering a great deal from the miserable conditions, excessive heat, and bad food, Antonio was released in a very weak and sickly condition. Throughout her incarceration, Major Williard begged her to sign the oath of loyalty to the Union and after much pleading by Williard and personal soul-searching by Antonio, she countered by asking him to resign his commission in exchange for her signing the oath. While the medicine was bitter, he agreed.

Following these actions, the two were married on March 10, 1864, in the great parlor of the Metropolitan Hotel in Washington, DC, amid an assemblage of admiring friends. After a honeymoon in Philadelphia and New York, they returned to their magnificent residence at Fourteenth and "G" Streets in Washington, DC. Antonio, however, never fully recovered from her many months of incarceration and she died just seven short years after her wedding day. Her spouse mourned his loss until his death in 1897, spending his last days as a recluse in their large home.[20]

Belle Boyd

The Confederate spy, Belle Boyd (May 9, 1814-June 11,1900), daughter of a Martinsburg, Virginia storekeeper, began her career as a secret agent at the age of seventeen. The Federal occupation of Martinsburg on July 3, 1861, drew Belle into free lance espionage and thus began her life of danger.

On July 4, 1861, a number of intoxicated soldiers were destroying private property in the town of Martinsburg. As the liquor flowed, bullets were fired through doors and windows and furniture was hurled into the streets. Women and children were rudely cursed, and when the drunken soldiers learned that Belle's room was decorated with "rebel" flags, they stormed the Boyd house. A quick-thinking Negro servant destroyed the flags before the soldiers found them and when the soldiers were unable to locate them, they hoisted a Federal flag over the residence to indicate submission by the occupants. When Mrs. Boyd quietly protested, a Union soldier became offensive in actions and language toward her. Consequently, Belle, with great audacity, drew her derringer and shot the offending soldier. His comrades carried him away, but he died within a short time.

The report of a Southern lady killing a Northern soldier caused quite a stir at Federalist headquarters. An investigation followed but she was acquitted and the event inevitably marked a turning point in Belle Boyd's life.[21] Despite her youthful age, she was feared by the Federalist as a dangerous foe. They attempted to keep her under strict surveillance, but she was unconcerned with her Union watchdogs. Her beauty and vivacious manner helped her lure secrets from her admirers and guards alike. Few military men could refrain from conversing freely with such a lovely young woman, and none sought to find her ulterior motives.

She sent her information to the closest Confederate leader via Negro and white messengers. Her best courier was the trustworthy Negro maid, Eliza, who had burned Belle's flags earlier. Eliza carried messages ingeniously written on eggs, legible only when held to a coal-oil lantern; sown in the soles of her shoes; packed in a loaf of bread; in the hollowed out centers of fruit; and in the hollow head of a doll.[22] Unfortunately, Belle's inexperience in transmitting information led to the Union's discovery of her activity for which she was sternly reprimanded. For Belle, however, her amateur efforts were just the beginning.

When the first Battle of Manassas took place she was at Front Royal,

Virginia, staying with relatives. Although she had a job in a hospital, Belle longed for a position as a courier. By autumn 1861, she received the appointment she desired with the Confederate Intelligence Service. As a courier for Generals Beauregard and Jackson, Miss Boyd was able to use her excellent horsemanship and knowledge of the Shenandoah Valley to her advantage.

Early in 1862, she was arrested upon suspicion and taken to Baltimore where she was released after a week of courteous imprisonment. She returned to Virginia, content for a time to visit with an aunt in Front Royal. While staying in there, the boarding house where she lived was often occupied by Union officers. She used this to her advantage by hiding in upstairs or next-door rooms and listening through knot holes in the floors and walls in an attempt to gain information for General Jackson. On one particular occasion, she huddled in a small upstairs closet all night and peered down a hole in the floor, straining her ears and eyes to gain Union secrets which she would rush to the Southerners. [23]

While at Front Royal, Miss Boyd performed her most notable service to the Confederacy. On May 23, 1862, General Stonewall Jackson prepared to recapture the Federally-held town of Front Royal as part of his drive against General Bank's Union forces. Belle, through her journey from Baltimore to Front Royal, her association with Union officers, and a recent message to her from an unknown source in Winchester, learned much about the strength and location of Northern troops. With her additional information, it was possible that Jackson, by hastening his attack, could save Front Royal's bridges scheduled for destruction by the retreating Union forces. This triggered her decision to reach Jackson immediately. As his troops approached, Miss Boyd, not wasting time to saddle her horse, raced on foot from Front Royal in a "conspicuous dark blue dress and fancy white apron" across the gap separating the two armies. [24] Although she was in range of the Union artillery and rifles, Belle breathlessly delivered her message to a staff officer, Henry Kyd Douglas. Whether her actions determined the maneuver's success is questionable but the bridges were saved and Jackson swept northward almost to Washington, DC. Later Belle received a note which read:

May 23, 1862

Miss Belle Boyd,
    I thank you, for myself and for the Army, for the immense service that you rendered your country today. Hastily, I am your friend, T. J. Jackson, C.A.S. [25]

The incident was widely publicized and Belle Boyd, already famous in the South, became notorious in the North. Union surveillance around Front

Belle Boyd in her Confederate gray after the war.

Royal tightened around Belle. On July 29, 1862, detectives from the United States Secret Service in Washington, under orders from Secretary of War Edwin Stanton, arrested Belle. The detectives escorted her to the Old Capitol Prison where she was incarcerated without specific charges. A month later, she was released in a general exchange of prisoners of war and returned to Richmond, Virginia.

During the next few months, Belle Boyd basked in the Southern reception of her deeds as a heroine. The following June she returned to Martinsburg to visit her ailing mother, shortly after the Confederate drive that ended at Gettysburg. When the Union troops returned to Martinsburg in July, she was again placed under arrest; in August, she was again taken to Washington and confined in the Old Capitol Prison. The agony of this stint was intensified by a severe case of typhoid fever but, nevertheless, she was released in December 1863, and banished to the South for the duration of the war. [26]

After recovering from the fever, she set out on what would be her final mission for the Confederacy. In March 1864, at twenty years of age, she left Richmond for London, carrying Confederate dispatches under the guise of recovering her health. The steamer on which she traveled was captured by a Union blockade vessel and she again became a prisoner, and was sent to Boston. Two noteworthy events followed this capture: she was banished to Canada, under punishment of death if recaptured, and she became engaged to Samuel W. Hardinge, Jr., the Union naval officer who took command of the Anglo-rebel steamer. Belle sailed from Canada to England, and her report to the British Confederacy agent was that she had destroyed the dispatches when the blockade-runner was seized and thus ended her service for the cause.

On August 25, 1864, Miss Boyd and Captain Hardinge were married in England where he had followed her after his dismissal from the United States Navy. Hardinge returned to the United States sometime after the wedding and was arrested and imprisoned until February, 1865. He returned to England after his release in poor health and died shortly thereafter. [27]

Hardinge was the first of three men to marry Miss Boyd. Her death occurred while she was married to Nathaniel Rue High on June 11, 1900. She died of a sudden heart attack and was interred in the Kilbourne Cemetery at Wisconsin Dells, Wisconsin. Appropriately, four Union veterans lowered her coffin into a grave bearing the following marker:

BELLE BOYD
Confederate Spy
Born in Virginia
Died in Wisconsin

Erected by a Comrade [28]

Elizabeth Van Lew

Virginia-born Unionist and Federal agent, Elizabeth Van Lew (October 17, 1818-September 25, 1900) held strong antislavery views long before the Civil War began. Many attributed these attitudes to Elizabeth's childhood training. Born in 1818, Elizabeth attended school in Philadelphia where her grandfather served as mayor for many years. The young student acquired an undying hatred for slavery, although she did not recognize the Negro people as equals and would not tolerate any familiarity on the part of her Negro servants. In the early 1850s she and her mother freed their house servants and one, Mary Elizabeth Bowser, was sent north for an education. Reportedly, they also purchased and then freed members of their servants' families in other households.

When the war came, Miss Van Lew remained openly loyal to the Union. The citizens of Richmond could not believe a true Virginia aristocrat would uphold such anti-slavery sentiments. Surely, they felt, such a person must have a touch of insanity, so they began calling her "Crazy Betsy," "Crazy Bet," or "Crazy Liz." Such appellations proved to be a valuable asset to her work as a spy during the Civil War. [29]

Elizabeth was a forty-three year old spinster when the war began in 1861. She kept up an endless line of correspondence with her friends in the North until postal communications became impossible; she then sent her correspondence through trusted couriers, mostly freed Negro slaves. She also developed a secret cipher which was placed in her watch and aided her in maintaining secrecy in her messages. (It was found among her possessions when she died.) Occasionally she would carry messages herself, disguised as an old farm woman with her farm basket on her arm, and her secrets safely hidden beneath the vegetables. As the war progressed, she began to hollow out the cores of the vegetables and fruit and hide the messages inside.

In her search for information, Elizabeth frequently visited Libby Prison, Castle Thunder, or the Belle Isle prisons. In order to slip messages in and out, she hid the ciphers in clothing, books, tobacco, food, or medicine and took them to Federal inmates. The books loaned to the prisoners were often returned with meaningful words underlined. Sometimes she would implement the use of an old-fashioned metal platter with a double bottom for conveying important documents. The platter would be filled with hot

Elizabeth Van Lew.

Libby Prison, Richmond, Va.

Castle Thunder Prison (above) and a silent sentinel on Belle Isle (below), with the James River and the city of Richmond in the background.

foods and the secrets were safely hidden in the bottom compartment; the guards never inspected the hot bottom of the platter. [30] When "Crazy Bet" was refused entrance to the prisons because the Confederates believed she was consorting with the enemy, she put on her prettiest dress and paraded in front of the provost marshal's office, turning on the charm, until her request for entrance was granted.

Due to her high social standing she was able to operate without too much interference. Her contacts extended into the Confederate government, and even into the Southern Capitol where she had strategically placed Mary Elizabeth Bowser as a maid.[31] Elizabeth was a familiar figure in Richmond, flitting about the Confederate capital mumbling meaningless words to herself and always keeping her ears open for any valuable information.

In her mansion she had an end room with its windows heavily curtained with quilts. The room was kept prepared for prison refugees who straggled in, and gas lights were kept burning continually to "throw dust in the eyes of suspicious persons." [32] On February 2, 1864, one hundred inmates escaped from Libby Prison through a tunnel, and General Straight was given a special hiding place in Elizabeth's attic.

Although the house was searched several times, neither the room nor the attic hiding place were ever found. They were not discovered until many years after the war, along with the secret post office that she had hidden in her sitting room where she kept many of her secret messages. The room contained a large fireplace with iron pilasters on either side, capped with crouched lion figures. One of these caps could be raised, like the lid of a box, and the hollow space beneath served as a safe. She would place messages in the safe and they would later be taken by a trusted Negro to Federal officers.

Of all the secret dispatches Elizabeth sent through Confederate lines, only one has survived to the present time. This was the ciphered dispatch (which inspired the abortive Kilpatrick-Dahlgren raid of March 1, 1864) she sent to General Benjamin Butler while he was headquartered at Fortress Monroe. The document was written in invisible ink and was visible only when the paper was dipped in milk. The message was as follows:

It is intended to remove Federal prisoners to Georgia, butchers, and bakers to go at once. They are already notified and selected. Quaker knows this to be true. Beware new and rash counsel. This I send you by directions of all our friends.

No attempt should be made with less than 30,000 cavalry, from 10,000 to 15,000 infantry...Hake and Kemper's brigades gone to North Carolina. Pickett's in or near Petersburg. Three regiments of cavalry disbanded by General Lee for want of horses. Morgan applying for 1000 choice men for a raid. [33]

The Van Lew Mansion, Richmond, Va.

Miss Van Lew's most daring exploit involved the disinterment of Colonel Ulric Dahlgren who was killed during Kilpatrick's raid on Richmond in February 1864. The Union officers, furnished with Confederate intelligence information supplied by Elizabeth, decided to liberate the Libby Prison inmates. The plan was devised by General Judson Kilpatrick and Colonel Dahlgren, but Dahlgren was ambushed and killed. The Confederates found papers on the deceased stating that he intended to burn Richmond and assassinate President Jefferson Davis. In turn, the body was publicly humiliated, clad in a rough garment, and buried secretly. Van Lew, however, was convinced that the papers were forgeries and proposed the spiriting away of Dahlgren's body for delivery to his family. After her agents located the grave, the body was exhumed and secretly taken to a loyalist's farm for a proper reburial. The revelation of the conspirators of this disentombment would have led to serious consequences since the public view of the deceased was less than favorable. [34]

As the Union forces approached Richmond late in 1864, Van Lew's espionage efforts peaked. To thwart public suspicion of her work, she prepared a room for General McClellan, leader of the Union forces several months before he was even expected. The townsfolk thought she had lost her mind, but once again she used public opinion to her benefit.

She used several methods to transmit her messages to Union forces and a series of five relay stations were established between the Chief of the Military Information Bureau and the Army of the Potomac at City Point. She had no difficulty in securing passes from the unsuspecting Confederate provosts for her servants to travel from her home to the Van Lew farm below Richmond, where the first relay station was. The messages were sent in egg shells, concealed in the baskets of produce, and the shoe soles of former Negro servants. A young seamstress, used as a courier, transported messages hidden among her patterns and yard goods. It is said that loyalist commanders received fresh flowers from her garden on the day she cut them.

With the fall of Richmond in April 1865, Elizabeth enjoyed her greatest moment in the sun. General Grant posted a guard at her home and Federal officers called on her to pay their respects to the Loyalist heroine. She was successful in her aid to the Federal cause and rejoiced in the glory of the

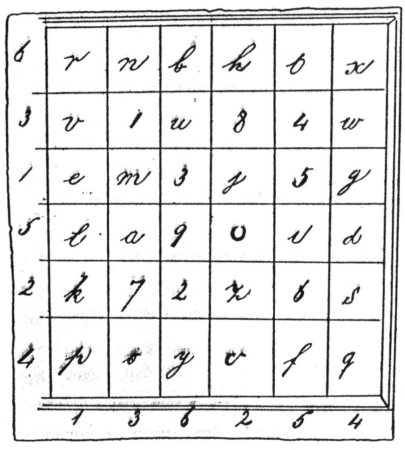

The 36-box cipher grid used by Elizabeth Van Lew to encode her secret messages.

Confederate defeat.[35]

When Grant became president, Miss Van Lew was appointed post-mistress of Richmond, a position she was forced to relinquish when Grant left his office. She was, however, appointed a clerk in the Post Office Department for sentimental reasons, but her peculiarities made her a liability to the organization. Miss Van Lew was reduced to the lowest clerk level which humiliated her, but her financial difficulties forced her to swallow her pride and remain on the job. She finally resigned when a newspaper described her as a "troublesome relic." [36]

A colonel, whom she had aided at Libby Prison, raised funds for her and saved her from total financial disaster. Her last years were spent as a recluse in the Church Hill mansion of her family in Richmond, Virginia, shunned by her Southern neighbors. When she died on September 25, 1900, at the age of eighty-two, she was buried in Shockhoe Hill Cemetery. The epitaph on her headstone is a tribute that she would have appreciated:

She risked everything that is dear to man—friends, fortune, comfort, health, life itself, all for one absorbing desire of her heart—that slavery might be abolished and the Union preserved. [37]

Sarah Emma Edmonds

Canadian-born Sarah Emma Evelyn Edmonds (December, 1841-September 5, 1898) fled to the United States in an attempt to escape an over-bearing father who had arranged her marriage to a local farmer twice her age. To travel without suspicion, she disguised herself as Franklin Thompson and obtained a job selling Bibles for a Hartford, Connecticut, publishing firm. Her travels took her to Michigan where "Frank Thompson" became friends with William R. Morse. Both enlisted in Company F of the Second Michigan Regiment of Volunteer Infantry and by June 1861, Edmonds, alias Thompson, was on the Virginia front. She witnessed the Battle of Bull Run but did not participate in any action until the Battle of Blackburn's Ford. Sarah's service as a spy began under her commanding officer, General McClellan.

Her initial experiences as a spy behind Confederate lines were in the guise of "Ned, the darkie." The young woman covered her face and hands with walnut stain topped with silver nitrate which turned her skin a gray-black color. She donned slave clothing and a black wig to cover her cropped hair and slipped through the Confederate lines on a damp, cold, moonless night. The following morning, she helped the other slaves carry breakfast to the Confederate soldiers and accompanied them to Yorktown to work on the building of the Rebel fortifications. The work ended at sunset, and Emma (as "Ned") was free to inspect the breastwork and cannons. Sketching the fortifications with blistered, calloused hands was difficult but she managed to note the size, quantity, and position of the mounted guns. She then concealed the papers under the inner sole of her shoes. [38]

Assigned to carry water to the officers, she was able to mingle long enough to gather the camp gossip from which she learned the number of reinforcements, both present and anticipated, and also where they were coming from. She heard that Yorktown was to be evacuated soon, which was the precise information she sought to acquire.

On the evening of her third day as "Ned," Emma made a dash for the Union line. She was spotted by a Confederate officer and was assigned guard duty and issued a rifle. As day broke, she filtered through a thicket to the safety of the Union line and the welcome sight of "Old Glory." Reporting to her commanding officer, she produced her sketches and turned in the Confederate rifle. Congratulations were in order and the rifle was sent to the War Department in Washington. While the information carried by Emma is questionable as to the expediting of Yorktown's evacuation, it is still considered some of the most useful information collected by a Union agent.

Emma undertook nine other espionage adventures. Her life was in constant danger because the countryside teemed with Southern loyalists, spies, and copperheads, but she remained true to her beliefs.

On one occasion, a leading merchant of Louisville, Kentucky, an outspoken Southern supporter, hired Emma (disguised as a young man) as a clerk. Most of his employees, fearing Union retaliation, left his employ but Emma was personable and efficient, and proved to have a head for business. She suggested the peddling of sundries to the soldiers, an idea to which the merchant readily agreed, and within two weeks, she was securing intelligence materials including the location of three Southern spies in the Union ranks.

Instinctively, Emma sought to entrap the closest Southern spy. She, disguised as the the clerk, told the merchant that she felt compelled to join the Confederate Army. Since Louisville was in Union hands, the merchant secured the services of a "Union" man to take her to the Confederate lines. Ironically, this man was actually a Confederate spy who had taken the Union oath of allegiance. The move was scheduled for the following night.

Emma volunteered for one final peddling expedition and the provost marshal was contacted to secure a travel permit. When the provost wandered into the store later that day, she slipped him a note and thus the trap was set. The "Union" man also came into the merchant's establishment that day and to Emma's surprise, was a well-known Louisville resident who was highly respected and without suspicion.

As evening approached, Emma and her escort headed southward. He spoke openly, almost boastfully, of his secret service activities, and the identity and exact locations of the other two spies were revealed in his glowing discourse. One spy was a sundries peddler, and the second was a photographer of Union officers. While in the middle of his recitation, a troop of Union soldiers engulfed the camp and the agent was caught in the trap. Rebel papers were found in his possession, leaving no doubt that he was indeed a Southern informant. He was executed at daybreak, and the peddler was captured and also killed. Having been forewarned, the photographer fled to the safety of the Confederacy. [39]

Emma used various disguises during her espionage attempts. For example, she infiltrated Confederate positions posing as an Irish peddler woman, complete with a basket of cakes, pies, and a thick Irish brogue. On another adventure, she used a mustard plaster to burn her face which was then colored with red ink and black pepper so she could pose as a grieving widow. [40] Eventually, however, after years of stress-filled service to the

The Battle of Williamsburg, Virginia, May 5, 1862.

Union, she became weak and sickly. In the disguise of Frank Thompson, she fought in the Battles of Williamsburg, Fair Oaks, Richmond, Antietam, and Fredericksburg. She fell ill at Vicksburg early in 1863 while she was in the guise of a male nurse. Fearing her secret would be revealed, Emma deserted on April 22; she resumed her female identity and worked as a nurse until the war ended.

Emma's secret was never revealed until she attended a regimental reunion without her disguise. (She had gotten married sometime previously, and was now Mrs. Linus H. Seelye.) Her fellow troop mates urged her to file for a veteran's pension and the case was taken to Congress; ironically, the senators were more interested in charging her with desertion. In the end, the desertion charges were dropped and she was granted a monthly pension of twelve dollars.

She suffered the remainder of her life from malaria and partial paralysis, which resulted from her escapades for the Union, and she died in LaPorte, Texas, in 1898. However, prior to her demise, Emma was mustered into the George B. McClellan Post Number Nine of the Grand Army of the Republic in Houston. She was the only female to be regularly received into the G.A.R. according to the Texas Parade, April 1958, in an article entitled "Footnote to History, The Last Years of Emma Edmonds."

Pauline Cushman

Born Harriet Wood (1833-1893), Mademoiselle Pauline Cushman acted in the grand tradition of a European spy-actress, speaking for one side and acting on behalf of the other. Her espionage career began in Louisville, Kentucky, when she was offered three hundred dollars to propose a toast to the Confederacy on stage; at the time, Louisville was under Union control. Before accepting the bet, she consulted the Union provost marshal who urged her to comply with the request and launched her into an espionage career. She came closer to being executed than any other female during the Civil War.

When she made her toast, the Southerners cheered and a brawl erupted. Numerous people were arrested by Union officers, including Pauline, and although her arrest was used to maintain her cover, she was fired from the theater company and forced to continue as a free agent-actress. [41] She identified with Southern sympathizers by using the story that she was searching for her rebel brother.

Her seductive manner made it easy for her to find company with Confederate officers, and she used those opportunities to learn as much as possible about the actions of the army. During one particular outing with Confederate Captain Blackman, she was invited to become his personal aide-de-camp. Although she politely refused his offer, Blackman had a trim gray officer's uniform made for her. Later captured in possession of this uniform, they were both arrested and tried as spies, but during the trial, Pauline was so ill from exposure that she could not rise from her bed. Her jailer, Captain Pedden, kept her advised of the situation and her life was saved when Union General Rosecrans launched an assault on Shelbyville where she was being held. [42]

When the Union troops learned Pauline was a spy for their cause, they showered her with candies, flowers, and other delicacies. Her only request was to be back inside the Union lines, and therefore, on a damp June day in 1863, her wish was granted. An ambulance was sent to transport her and two generals carried her to the vehicle in a chair while a major sheltered her from the rain by holding an umbrella over her head. She resided in Nashville where she suffered severe bouts of depression. The Union paid for her hospital care and Rosecrans and other Union officers visited her often. These men testified to her meritorious acts and had her declared a major in

Major Pauline Cushman.

the cavalry. The grateful Union presented her with a trim military habit, and from that time forward, she chose to be called "Miss Major Cushman." [43]

When her health improved, she returned to the stage as a well-celebrated monologist describing her espionage experiences. However, her life deteriorated after a series of unsuccessful marriages, faded beauty, and a nation tired of her story. She eventually became a morphine addict and committed suicide. In a fitting contradiction to the failure of the government to provide her with a pension, the veterans of the Grand Army of the Republic spared her a pauper's grave. Escorted by a troop of Union veterans, "The Spy of Cumberland" was given a military funeral with a large white coffin surrounded by thousands of flowers. She went to her grave on December 6, 1893 with flags, an honor guard, and a rifle salute: a ceremony worthy of her service.

Anna Ella Carroll

A unique contribution was made to the Union cause by Anna Ella Carroll (August 29, 1815-February 19, 1893). Anna, the oldest child of Thomas King Carroll and Juliana (Stevenson) Carroll of Kingston Hall, Maryland, was tutored in legal affairs and other standard courses such as reading, writing, and mathematics by her father. When he was elected governor of Maryland in 1829, Anna moved with him to Annapolis, leaving her mother and younger sisters and brothers at Kingston Hall. This was the point in her life that she developed her strong nationalist position. By the time she was fifteen, she was a spirited redhead, whom the Maryland social set nicknamed "Princess Anne." [44]

By 1830 the supporting of two households, one in Annapolis and the second in Kingston Hall, took its financial toll on the Carrolls. The family was forced to move to a smaller residence in Cambridge, Massachusetts. At this point, Anna began writing anonymously on political subjects, and had a major portion of her income forwarded to her parents. Her staunchest writings were on behalf of the Know-Nothing party.

Her political background prepared her for the next phase of her life—the Civil War. Her writing ability drew the attention of President Lincoln and his cabinet members, and Assistant Secretary of War Thomas A. Scott commissioned her to write and publish ten thousand copies of a pamphlet entitled *The Reply*. This document strongly criticized the secession of the Southern states and was followed by two more pamphlets entitled *The War Powers of the General Government* (1861) and *The Relation of the National Government to the Revolted Citizens Defined* (1862). The documents were produced at the request of President Lincoln and they argued that secession was unconstitutional and the formation of the Confederacy an act of rebellion. [45]

Her most important contribution to the Federal service was an espionage expedition she made to St. Louis, Missouri, in August 1861, on presidential orders. She and her traveling companion, Lemuel Evans, were sent to scout the Confederate fortifications in the area, as well to carry information to the Union officials stationed there. The documents were dispatched to the appropriate officers and the scouting trip was completed uneventfully. However, while traveling on the Mississippi in an attempt to gain additional information concerning the Confederates, Anna encountered an old ship's

Anna Ella Carroll.

captain named Winfred Scott who allowed her to peruse his river charts and maps. After which, she surveyed the plot charts of the Tennessee River and hatched a plan with the assistance of Scott and Evans.

Anna and Evans returned to Washington, DC, in late November 1862, carrying the collected information, as well as a plan for ending the war. It was during the discussion of the fortifications that Anna uncovered her plan to send the Union army up the Tennessee River, which flows backward from the sea. The idea was so preposterous that Lincoln ordered his war department to convene. His generals scoffed at the proposal, especially since a woman had devised it but the plan was later implemented by Lincoln's War Department and the credit for it went to Ulysses Grant. [46]

Anna filed a claim with the government for her expedition expenses as well as the sixty thousand dollars that Lincoln promised her for the plan. He also promised her a commission which would have given her a lifelong pension, but an assassin's bullet killed Lincoln and squashed Anna's claim. Congress rejected her claim and her commission even though she had documentation supporting her cause.

For several years, she protested to Congressmen while supporting herself as a pamphleteer and railroad attorney. Her last plea before Congress was in 1880 and she fought back with her final brochure North American Review (1886) in which she blasted male injustice. She died in 1893 at the age of 77 in Washington, DC, an impoverished, embittered woman who was denied her one great honor, that of saving the Union.

Hattie Lawton

Although little is known about Hattie Lawton (?-?), she was one of the Union's most experienced operatives and perhaps their best female agent. Hattie was assigned to Baltimore, a Southern sore on the Union side, where she worked with Timothy Webster in securing rebel information.

In January 1862, during an espionage excursion to Richmond, Webster became ill and Lawton was forced to care for him. Having to remain in one town for several weeks was dangerous for an operative, and while there they were directed to report to the Confederate General Winder. During a visit to Winder's office, the pair was recognized by a Confederate spy whom they had arrested earlier, and the two were arrested on the spot. Hattie was tried and sentenced to a year in Carroll Prison. She tried desperately to get the death sentence of her partner commuted, to the point of even requesting audience with President and Mrs. Jefferson Davis, but she was unsuccessful and Webster was executed. Hattie was released in 1863 and she then slipped into anonymity. Her later life and demise are sheer speculation. [47]

Hattie Lawton pleading for the life of Federal spy, Timothy Webster.

Laura Ratcliffe

The young and beautiful Laura Ratcliffe (?-?) lived with her mother and two sisters on a small farm near Frying Pan, Virginia, when the Civil War started. Laura first drew attention to herself by nursing fallen Confederate soldiers in her area and even General J.E.B. Stuart was taken with her dark brown eyes, shining ebony hair, and shapely figure as she consoled the wounded. (He later dedicated poetry to Laura along with a gold watch and chain.) However, it was General Stuart who was instrumental in making the Ratcliffe-Mosby connection.

Mosby used the Ratcliffe residence as his headquarters. It was also used as a depository for confiscated Yankee materials until they could be safely turned over to the proper Southern authorities. Laura, herself repeatedly carried messages to and from Mosby safely hidden in the false bottom of her egg basket. [48]

On one occasion, Ranger Mosby was saved from certain death by Laura's quick thinking. A large band of Northern soldiers were hidden near Frying Pan, lying in wait for the Ranger. Upon the intrusion of Mosby's forces into the Yankee picket line, the larger force of soldiers would fall on the Confederate troopers and kill them or take them prisoner. Laura heard of the plan and warned Mosby, who reversed his intentions and, in turn, captured the Yankee soldiers who had intended on being the captors.

At war's end, Laura lived in an impoverished state with her invalid sister on a poverty-stricken and war-ravaged farm. The fences were broken from cannon balls, and weeds controlled the fields and pastures. The once fertile farmland was hardened by repeated traffic of the Northern and Southern cavalry, and survival was nearly impossible. She was rescued by a generous, elderly Yankee neighbor named Milton Hannah, who offered to build a house for them near his own so that he and his mother could help Laura care for her sister. Laura consented and he built her a beautiful two story home near a brook; thus, the residence was called "Brookside." After the death of her invalid sister, Laura and Milton were married and resided at Brookside.

Upon the death of her husband, Laura was left a wealthy woman, inheriting a very large estate with abundant monetary backing. She devoted much of her wealth to the poor and the destitute, and much of the Brookside property was deeded to the Presbyterian and Methodist churches, even though she professed to be an Episcopalian. At the age of 79, an accident occurred while she was feeding chickens. She fell in the mud and broke her ankle but the break did not heal properly. Laura spent the last years of her life in solitude as a semi-invalid and she died at the age of eighty-seven. [49]

James Ewell Brown (JEB) Stuart.

Clara Judd

Love sometimes intervened in espionage affairs, and such was the case with Mrs. Clara Judd (?-?), the widow of an Episcopal clergyman. Mrs. Judd had quite a reputation as a Confederate spy and smuggler, the latter being her claim to fame because she supplied most of the drugs used by the Tennessee army.

On December 16, 1862, Mrs. Judd was sent to Louisville for the purpose of gathering information concerning the size and disposition of the Federal troops stationed there. While walking between Murfeesborough and Nashville, she was approached by a paroled Union man named Delos Thurman Blythe. Blythe was actually a Yankee agent sent by Allen Pinkerton, in charge of the Union detectives, to trap her. But, using all of his guile, he soon won Mrs. Judd's confidence. As they walked, he explained that he was an agent for the Confederacy, describing in detail several of his exploits, and by the time the couple reached Nashville, Clara was chattering about her espionage and smuggling experiences, completely unaware of her companion's intentions. When they reached Nashville, the pair found accommodations at the Commercial Hotel, and once settled into their separate suites, Blythe contacted the Federal authorities and asked them to keep her under constant surveillance.

Blythe continued to pamper Mrs. Judd throughout her stay in Nashville and simultaneously learned more about her spy tactics each day. Meanwhile, the surveillance team noted every move she made. When she made an effort to move on to another location, Blythe faked a severe illness which required a nurse and, of course, Clara remained and nursed her lover back to health. The "illness" gave Blythe the time he needed to set up the final act of his trap.

When he had fully recovered from his "illness," Blythe joined Clara as she prepared to depart Nashville. She talked about packing the medicines, drugs, and secret documents in the false bottoms of her traveling trunks, but Blythe told her not to worry because he had taken care of everything. He told her that her baggage would not be searched. At that point, Clara should have been suspicious of his actions, but she was preoccupied with her love for him.

The train had scarcely left Nashville when it was ordered to be stopped by Federal agents; Clara and Blythe were arrested and their property seized.

According to pre-laid plans, Blythe was roughed up, which distressed Clara more than her own arrest. The Federals lodged Clara in a Nashville hotel while Blythe was taken to the Federal prison. Believing Blythe would quickly be executed, Clara begged audience with the Federal authorities to speak on his behalf, and meanwhile, Blythe was released from custody. Clara never found out the fate of her lover, nor the fact that he had deceived her.

General Rosencrans ordered Clara Judd sent to the Alton, Illinois military prison to await her trial. Since there were no women incarcerated there, Mrs. Judd was placed in a local boarding house at a cost of two dollars per week, which was paid by the government. She remained imprisoned there until August 4, 1863, when she was released without trial. Suffering both physically and from a lost love, she returned home and never saw Delos Blythe again. The tactics he employed on her cost the Confederate army a considerable amount in drugs and information, not to mention the fact that General Morgan's infamous raid into Kentucky was delayed due to her capture.[50]

The Moon Sisters

Ginnie (?-1926) and Lottie (?-?) Moon, the South's most authentic sister spy act, were the most unusual of the agents. Ginnie raised the South's war morale by getting herself engaged to sixteen boys at one time, and when questioned about the logic of such a risky situation, she retorted, "If they died in battle, they'd have died happy...and if they lived, I didn't give a damn." [51]

Lottie made romantic history in another way, due to her indecisiveness over a mate. A man, later famous as a Union officer, stood next to Lottie at the altar. When questioned if she took that man to be her husband, she paused and shouted, "No-siree-bob!" turned on her heel, and marched from the church. The jilted officer eventually had his chance for revenge, but when the Moon sisters stood (charged with espionage) before him, General Ambrose Burnside softened and released them.

Like many spies-in-the-making, the young Moon sisters performed in amateur theatricals. Lottie extended her expertise to ventriloquism and also had a trick jaw that allowed her to dislocate it at will, making a loud cracking sound at which time she would exhibit an expression of extreme agony.

Their first taste of espionage came when Walker Taylor, an undercover agent for the South, asked them to carry a message from General Sterling Price to General Edmund Kerby-Smith in Kentucky. He could not carry the document himself because he was under Federal surveillance and was sure that he would be caught. Within the hour, the girls left as bent old women, draped in shabby, moth-eaten shawls and bonnets. Later that afternoon, they crossed the Ohio River by ferry and located transportation to carry them to Lexington.

At this point, they changed their disguises and became Irish women. Although refused travel permits by the officials, their grieving-Irish-widow's act touched the hearts of several "fellow Irish (shore) men" who smuggled them aboard the transport ship on which they worked. Once in Lexington, they thanked the Irishmen and depended on luck. Luckily, fate played into their hands. The first person the girls met was Colonel Thomas Scott. Lottie thrust the document into his hands with and commanded him to "promise...[he would] give these to Colonel Kerby-Smith, and nobody else." [52] Although shocked by the girls' disguises, he agreed.

Ambrose E. Burnside.

Later that evening, the girls left Lexington by train for a point near their home, still dressed as mournful little Irish women. While on the train, a warning was issued to watch for a "female spy." Again they turned on the tears, this time deceiving a fellow coachmate, Union General Leslie Coombs, pouring out the poor widows' stories (accented with starving children at home details), and the General took them to heart and saw them safely off the train at their destination point. From that location they walked across fields and through woods and arrived home in time for breakfast.

Lottie's next major assignment came about because of her association with Louisville Presbyterian editor, Dr. Stuart Robinson. A staunch advocate of the South, the minister wrote seething articles against the Union. When a "price was placed on his head," Robinson escaped to Canada and while there, he helped to stir up Southern sentiments. At that time, the Canadian Confederates could make great use of a competent agent such as Lottie Moon.

A plan was devised with Lottie pretending to be a British subject seeking to mend her delicate health. Traveling with forged papers, she arrived in Washington, DC, with few difficulties. The deception was so perfect that even Secretary of War Edwin M. Stanton, "the suspicious one," was convinced by Lottie's act. She was invited to join President Lincoln's party when they reviewed the Army of the Potomac at Fredericksburg, and she secured a pass for Virginia and rode off quietly.

She had delivered all of the messages to her Southern cohorts by the time Stanton got wind of the ruse, and she continued to collect data as she worked her way home. She encountered her first serious difficulty near Winchester in the Shenandoah Valley. Union General F. J. Milroy listened to Lottie's act with the variation of being confused and going to the wrong Hot Springs, and she begged him for a pass through the lines. General Milroy decided to involve his personal surgeon in Lottie's illness and thus investigate her situation further.

At the army hospital, Lottie pretended to be so ill she could not leave her carriage. The surgeon had two of his men lift her from the carriage and carry her into the hospital in a straight backed chair. As the doctor examined her, she explained that her rheumatism had affected her heart. Crying at the doctor's touch, she performed the best acting of her life; she even paled with false agony. True to form, she then dislocated her trick jaw writhing in pain. The pompous doctor shook his head and noted that hers was truly a sad case. He commanded his orderlies to carry Lottie gently back downstairs to her waiting carriage. The general then granted her the pass and she was soon on her way home.[53]

Ginnie, in the meantime, had her own escapades. She was busy carrying messages to Nathan Bedford Forrest concerning the Union troop movements in the Memphis area. She was often captured but was arrested only once. The Memphis Commercial Appeal, the local newspaper, described her as follows:

> she needed no pass to get through the Union lines, her eyes and her way won her permission everywhere.[54]

In February, 1863, Confederate General Sterling Price had new and vital intelligence for Ohio officers. Ginnie volunteered to carry the messages, and with relatives in Ohio, she had an excuse for the trip. Since she could not be denied, the general agreed to let her go with the documents. The trip began in an ambulance accompanied by eight soldiers. At Memphis, she picked up her mother and they made their way casually to her brother-in-law's home near Oxford, Ohio.

After the messages were delivered, the two ladies prepared to board the *Alice Dean*, a cargo ship on which they had secured passage. Ginnie carried a secret dispatch for General Sterling in her bosom. Before the ship left harbor, Union officers entered the Moon stateroom and arrested the ladies for performing treasonous acts. The commanding officer, Captain Harrison Rose, demanded the ladies to submit to a physical search. At that moment,

Ginnie reached into her pocket and removed a Colt revolver which she leveled on the captain. She verbally lashed out at him and forced him to retreat from the stateroom with the luggage, keys, and his life. Ginnie quickly locked the door, pulled the dispatch from her bosom, dipped it in the water pitcher, and in three lumps swallowed it. When Captain Rose returned with assistants, the ladies were prepared to leave the stateroom.

They were escorted to the Union headquarters where their belongings were searched. Quilted garments and coverlets filled with opium, quinine, and morphine (drugs desperately needed in the South) were ripped open. Mrs. Moon quietly explained the need of the drugs for her sickly children. Their traveling attire was confiscated. By the next morning, Ginnie was wearing forty bottles of morphine, seven pounds of opium, and a quantity of camphor in the hems of her skirts and petticoats.

Before pardons and passes could be secured, the ladies had to appear before General Burnside. Burnside chastised the ladies for their activities but Ginnie looked him straight in the eyes and told him, "General, I have a little honor. I could not have let you know what I carried or what I did."[55] The general, obviously sympathetic, took the ladies' situation from the customhouse officers and handled it himself. While the two women were under house arrest in a Cincinnati hotel, the situation became more complicated.

In the meantime, the general had a British lady brought before him who requested a pass. General Burnside, who had courted Lottie Moon long enough to recognize every line in her face, immediately recognized her. She tried every scheme that she knew but none worked on the general and she soon joined her mother and sister under house arrest.

General Burnside kept the ladies in suspense for a long time, making every effort to frighten them out of their Confederate activities. He had rumors of trials and executions slipped to them almost daily and he had gossip spread of female operatives being spirited away into oblivion by Federal officers who did not wish them to face public execution. Although charges were never pressed, the ladies were held under surveillance for several months and were required to report daily to the general in Cincinnati. In the meantime, the younger Moons collected marriage proposals from the Yankee gentlemen, along with valuable information which was then slipped to convenient agents from the South, all the while appearing as gadflies to the Union.[56]

The ladies were eventually released and allowed to return home. Hoping to restrict their Confederate operations, the Union officers in Virginia required all three to report daily at ten in the morning to Federal General Hurlbert. This order did not last long because Ginnie and Lottie used the occasion to gain Union information. After three months of such reporting, the general commanded the Moon family to "get out and stay out!" The ladies picked up their skirts and whisked away.

Late in 1864, the girls received a letter from their brother who was ill from war wounds. He, his wife, and two children had escaped to Southern France and invited Lottie and Ginnie to join them. The two ladies and their mother obtained passes and made their way to Newport News, Virginia, where they were stopped by Union General Benjamin Butler. They were ordered to take the Union oath if they expected to continue on to France and, naturally, the ladies were indignant.

They were kept in custody for several months. Daily they were reminded that if they took the oath, they would be allowed to join the rest of their family in France. They told them that they might as well recant their Confederate convictions and take the oath because they would be forced to take it when Butler reached Richmond anyway. Ginnie gave a shriek and exclaimed, "If Butler's in Richmond, he'll be nailed to a tree."[57] That was the end of it. The ladies were escorted back to Confederate territory and not permitted to carry on with their journey.

The long war eventually ended and although the South lost, the Moon sisters never accepted defeat. Ginnie, who lived sixty years after Appomattox, was rambunctious as ever. She was a living anachronism in her herringbone shirt-waist silk dresses and tiny stylish hats. For a while she took in male boarders and was a heroine in the yellow fever epidemic of the 1870s. When she reached the age of seventy-five she discovered Hollywood. She confronted producer Jesse Lashy about a job and he asked her what made her think she could act. Ginnie stamped her foot, folded her small arms, and bluntly stated, "I'm seventy-five years old and I've acted all of them." The producer responded with a nod and said, "You'll do."[58] She starred with Polo Negri, Douglas Fairbanks, and Mary Miles Minter in various films. At seventy-six, she donned a padded jacket and helmet for a seaplane flight and in her later years, she took herself to Greenwich Village where she entertained the younger residents.

As one of her final deeds, she tamed a wild alley cat who became her constant companion. At her demise (in September 1926), the eighty-one year old Ginnie was found stretched on the floor with her cat; she had finally stopped fighting the Civil War.

Older sister Lottie became a novelist and pioneer newspaper correspondent. She covered the European capitals during the Franco-Prussian war but very little is known of Lottie's final exploits.

Loreta Janita Velazquez

Not all of the female spies in the Civil War lived in the United States. Loreta Janita Velazquez (1842-?) was born in Havana, Cuba. She was the daughter of Cuban aristocracy and was married at an early age to an American, living in Cuba, named Rouch. When the Civil War began, Rouch joined the Confederate army where he soon died in a firearms accident.

Grief-stricken, Loreta used her wealth to equip and command a company of cavalry for the Confederacy. She dressed as an officer and led her men into the Battles of Bull Run and Ball's Bluff in 1861. However, bored by the inactivity of military life, she soon left her troopers in the command of the provost marshal. She then decided to take matters into her own hands. She deceived an old Negro wash woman into giving her clothing to replace her Confederate uniform and told her that she was going to Washington to persuade them to free all the Negroes in the South. She gave the old woman a twenty dollar bill in exchange for a dress, shawl, sunbonnet, and shoes.

She lied and bribed her way across the region, often replacing her tattered clothing with some supplied by those sympathetic to her tales. She was so well-supplied with clothing that her arrival in Washington was unnoticed because she had the appearance of a normal travelling person. Procuring a room at the Brown Hotel, she began gathering information concerning the Federal movements in the Mississippi Valley and the role of the Union fleet. She also learned that there were openings in the Federal detective corps, Allan Pinkerton's group. Loreta was certain that she could supply important information to the Confederates if she could gain such employment.

She met with Lafayette C. Baker, chief detective of the Washington branch, and told him one of the biggest lies of her career. She informed him of her loyalty to the North and how she was sorely persecuted by the Confederates. Consequently, she became an agent to the Union without any trouble. Her first Federal assignment was to the Northwest Territory where she was to help quash an insurrection contrived by the Confederates in the forty prison camps. The Confederate authorities used the opportunity of her trip to transport messages and funds to their agents in Canada.

Loreta concocted a plan for Baker requesting his permission to pass herself off as a Confederate operative so that she might gain additional information about the Confederate high command's plans for the northwest. Although warned of the danger, she was granted the needed passes, given

The Battle of Ball's Bluff, Virginia (above), October 21, 1861, and the ruins of the Henry house on the 1st Manassas battlefield (below).

five thousand dollars in Confederate funds, and one hundred fifty Federal dollars. Traveling from Washington to Richmond was relatively easy, and after she acquired the valued Confederate dispatches, she was soon on her way to New York. Obviously Baker did not entirely trust her because he had a detective follow her once she returned to Federal territory.

Being forewarned by an associate as she disembarked the train from Richmond to New York, Loreta took pains to remain inconspicuous. Baker's man did not have a good description of her, so she could disguise herself easily. The agent was on the same train as Loreta as it left Rochester, but she wrapped a shawl about her head and assumed the role of an Irish woman. Ironically, the agent came and sat next to her and questioned her about her travels. He ended their conversation by producing a photo of Loreta and asking her if she had seen the woman in the photo, and of course, she denied it. She asked the agent if the lady was his wife, and, in turn, she received a recitation on his liability to his organization. Although she was thoroughly entertained by the conversation, she was relieved when the agent left to torment some other unsuspecting female on the train.

Loreta's arrival in Canada was relatively uneventful. Her visit to Johnson's Island posed some danger for her because it was possible for her guise as a Federal agent to be revealed. Her anxiety was soon eased when she realized that her disguise would be honored by the Confederates whom she had come to save. She dispatched the Rebel messages and monies to the proper authorities, and the proposed insurrection was scheduled for September 19, 1864. Unfortunately, an unhappy Rebel officer named Langhorn leaked out the details of the plan to Federal authorities and subsequently, the Rebel leaders were arrested just hours before the insurrection was to occur. Loreta, however, escaped unsuspected.[59]

Nancy Hart

Life for the Scotch-Irish Americans of the Tennessee Mountains was one of simple existence. Nancy Hart (?-?) was one of the uneducated but trail-wise youth of the area. She knew little of the world outside her own region, but she knew she was on the side of the war with the South. She frequently served as a guide for "rebel" detachments, leading them through the rugged terrain she knew so well, and she led the soldiers to isolated Yankee outposts where surprise was definitely on the side of the Confederates. She also often spied on the Northern troopers. By peddling eggs and vegetables at the Yankee strongholds, she would learn all that she could about the strengths of the Northern troops and their plans for attack. All this information was then stored in her mind and reported back to southern officers.

Nancy's one grave mistake was in allowing herself to be used too often. The Federal government soon placed a bounty on her head for espionage and treasonous practices and she was captured in July 1862, while on a scouting expedition to Summerville, Tennessee. Shortly thereafter, an inexperienced photographer attempted to photograph the notorious spy but she was frightened by both the camera and the photographer. After much harassment, however, the photographer was eventually successful.

During her captivity, Nancy wanted nothing more than a chance to get even with her captors. She soon overpowered her guard and fatally wounded him with his own musket. She then stole a horse belonging to the Yankee commanding officer and rode away into the dark night, heading for the nearest Confederate camp. The next morning, she led Major Bailey and two hundred men to Summerville. The Federal pickets were panic-stricken and fled without a shot. At four in the morning, the Yankees were awakened by a single shot, rushed into the commons area and found themselves surrounded by the Southern soldiers.

Bailey's men confiscated all of the Federal livestock, weapons, and ammunition. The Northern men were taken prisoner and marched down the same road they had forced Nancy to trod. In the end, Nancy Hart proved she was not just an ignorant mountain girl.[60]

Augusta Mason

Some of the Civil War spies relocated to aid their respective causes. Such was the case of Augusta Morris Mason (?-?), a gracious thirty-year-old widow who moved her family of two children from Richmond to Washington at the request of the Confederate hierarchy. They lived in the Brown Hotel where she protested the rebel actions vocally.

Detective Allan Pinkerton of the Federal Secret Service was suspicious of Augusta from the very beginning and considered her militarily dangerous. He and his men spied on her continually through the illness and death of her young son and even at the child's funeral. Two days after the funeral, a Federal general ordered Augusta's arrest and on February 7, 1862, she was arrested and sent to the Old Capitol Prison where Rose Greenhow was confined. This action posed another problem for Augusta because Rose was her mother-in-law and was exceptionally jealous of her. This led to several rumors being started concerning Augusta's ancestry, which were strongly denied, but Rose's feelings never changed toward Augusta. Obviously, even though these two women had much in common, they were bitter enemies.[61]

Augusta's imprisonment was made easier for her by the dispensing of small favors by her to prison authorities and fellow prisoners. Unlike Rose, whose notorious temper denied her any privileges, Augusta experienced considerable freedom while in prison. Still, she longed to be completely free.

On May 1, 1862, Augusta was brought before a review board composed of Judge Pierrepont and General John Dix where she portrayed the "helpless female" figure. She protested loudly to the authorities for the horrendous maltreatment she suffered while in prison. She also explained that her arrest was the direct result of lies started by Rose Greenhow. Ultimately, the examining officials recommended that she and her child be escorted to the Virginia state line and released after giving her word that she would not return to the North. Transportation was arranged for Augusta and her child and they reached Richmond on June 4 without tribulation. She soon traded her spy clothes for a nurse's uniform, and remained at this occupation until the end of the war.[62]

Eugenia Phillips

Eugenia Phillips (?-?), the wife of Phillip Phillips, a noted lawyer and former Alabama representative, was one of the most active Confederate spies in Washington. The fifty-year-old mother of nine was a close friend of Rose Greenhow and like her intimate friend, she entertained Washingtonians in lavish style. At these social affairs, gossip was exchanged and opinions were freely stated, even though the guests were often mixed Northerners and Southerners.

Eugenia and her unmarried sister, known only as Miss Levy, engaged in Confederate espionage in close cooperation with Rose Greenhow's ring. Frequently Eugenia would pass on Federal secrets to Confederate political and military officials. She is said to have forwarded messages of vital importance to General Beauregard at Manassas Junction, often sending them by young girls who hid the ciphered notes in their long hair.[63]

Mrs. Phillips' open advocacy of the Southern cause, in spite of her husband's efforts to quiet her, was the principal reason for her arrest, rather than her espionage efforts. Her open denunciation of the North was so profuse that Eugenia, her two younger daughters, and her sister were imprisoned, for a period of time, at "Fort Greenhow" with Rose Greenhow.

Eugenia's husband had powerful influences which were soon at work trying to relocate the vocal Mrs. Phillips and her family safely within the Confederate lines. Secretary of War Edwin M. Stanton and the Judge Advocate, Thomas M. Key, procured this relocation for Phillips. Shortly after Eugenia 's release from "Fort Greenhow," Rose Greenhow walked past her home with her guards. Eugenia went to an open window where Rose tossed in a ball of pink worsted yarn, saying,lightheartedly, "Here is your yarn. You left it at my house, Mrs. Phillips," and then made her way down the street chattering to her unknowing guards.

Eugenia knew that the yarn had a hidden meaning because she had not left it at Rose's house. Once safe behind the Confederate lines, she delivered the yarn ball to President Jefferson Davis and she found a ciphered message in its center.

Eugenia's most troublesome time was when General Benjamin Butler occupied New Orleans near where she and her family resided. In April 1862, Butler made a number of arrests, including that of Eugenia, whom he sentenced to solitary confinement on Ship Island. Ship Island was a narrow

Benjamin F. Butler.

ridge of sand, seven miles long and one-half mile wide, located ten miles from the Mississippi mainlands. The only buildings on the island were Butler's former headquarters and the yellow fever station on the western shore. She was held on the island for two and one-half months until the Southern dander forced Butler to concede her release. Upon her release she stated, "It [Ship Island] had one advantage over the city [New Orleans],sir; you were not there." and she further stated that "It is fortunate that neither the [yellow] fever nor General Butler is contagious."[65]

Once released from Ship Island, Eugenia and her family moved to Mobile, Alabama, where she was heralded as a true Southern heroine and was eulogized by the Confederate media. After the war, the Phillips family returned to Washington where her husband resumed his practice as one of the city's most outstanding lawyers. The rest of their lives continued with relative anonymity.

Rebecca Wright

Rebecca Wright, a quiet Quaker schoolmistress living in Winchester Virginia, was perhaps the most unsuspecting of the female spies. On September 15, 1864, General Phillip Sheridan wrote a message on a piece of fine tissue paper rolled tightly in a tin foil pellet. A Negro messenger was ordered to carry it to Rebecca Wright with the speculation that should the messenger be searched by the enemy, he could easily swallow the document. The note to Rebecca read as follows:

> I know from Major General Crook that you are a loyal lady and still love the old flag. Can you inform me of the position of Early's forces, the number of divisions in his army, and the strength of any or all of them and his probable represented intentions? Have any troops arrived from Richmond, or any more coming?
>
> I am very respectfully your obedient servant,
> P. H. Sheridan, Major General Commanding [66]

The messenger arrived at the Wright residence at about noon on September 16, 1864, stating that he had an important message for Rebecca. The frightened schoolmistress escorted the Negro into a room and closed the door. He retrieved the pellet from his mouth and deposited it in Rebecca's trembling hands. The Negro reminded her that the foil must be saved for her answer; he then told her that he would return in three hours for her reply.

Rebecca was terrified after the Negro left. Since she and her mother were known to be adherents to the Northern cause, their Confederate neighbors had little to do with them, and they feared knowledge of Rebecca's connection with General Sheridan might evoke physical hostilities.

Ironically, however, there was a Confederate officer recovering from his wounds and boarding at a house nearby. As a convalescent, he was allowed to wander about the community. Two days before Sheridan's note arrived, the officer had asked to call on Rebecca and she graciously allowed him to visit her after school.

During the course of their conversation, the wounded soldier revealed the location of Kershaw's division of infantry, and Cutshaw's battalion of artillery. At the time, Rebecca listened quietly, absorbing all the information and wondering how she would utilize it. When the request from Sheridan arrived, Rebecca knew exactly what she had to do.

She prepared her reply to Sheridan which stated:

> I have no communication whatever with the rebels, but I will tell you what I know. The division of General Kershaw and Cutshaw's artillery, twelve guns, and men, General Anderson, commanding, have been sent away and no more are expected to arrive as they can not be spared from Richmond. I do not know how the troops are situated. I will take pleasure here- after learning all I can of their strength and positions, and the bearer may call again.
>
> Very respectfully yours. [67]

The Negro arrived promptly at three o'clock that afternoon to pick up Rebecca's reply. Sheridan received the information that same day and he concluded that this was his opportunity to attack: he threw his whole army upon Early's weakened forces in Winchester.

Rebecca and her family were frightened by the noise of battle as they awoke on September 17, 1864. They hurriedly hid in the cellar as the fear of falling shells and Rebecca's connection with the Yankees were equal; eventually, as the noise of the battle subsided, the Wrights came from their shelter.

General Sheridan rode directly from the battlefield to Rebecca's front door to personally thank her for her part in his victory. She begged him not to mention her assistance, fearing her neighbors' retaliation, but he assured her the Confederates would not trouble her or her family.

Before he left the following day, Sheridan stopped by Rebecca's classroom to bid the young schoolmistress an affectionate goodbye. Once he left, life resumed its normal patterns for Rebecca Wright. She continued to teach a small group of children in Winchester, and all the while, her part in the Battle of Winchester remained a dark secret.

Early in January 1867, a letter and gift arrived from General Sheridan. The letter thanked Rebecca for her assistance in his victory at Winchester and on the back of the letter was an endorsement by General Grant recommending Rebecca to a treasury department position in appreciation for her services to the Union. The letter was accompanied by a gold watch. This evidence released Rebecca's secret to the public. The Union people gathered around her, ecstatic with pride, and most of the Winchester residents were wild with indignation. Her life became full of danger; rowdies heckled her on the street and young boys spit on her. Her boarding house was boycotted to the point that she was reduced to dire poverty, supported only by the meager income from her school house.

Two more years passed before she received Grant's appointment. Her Quaker friends urged Congress to grant her a pension for her devotion to

Philip H. Sheridan (left) and a post-Civil War view of Winchester, Va. (below).

the Union cause, but the request was denied. She finally received her position when Grant became President and the employment required a move to Washington, so Rebecca bid her students and friends in Winchester farewell. While employed with the treasury department, she married William C. Bonssall and retired from her post in 1914.

Among Rebecca's most cherished mementos were the gold watch and chain, Sheridan's letter with Grant's endorsement, and the crumpled tissue paper note that began her career as a spy. For many years she tried to locate the Negro that carried the message but she died never finding him.

Olivia Floyd

Olivia Floyd was born in 1832 on the Rose Hill Estate, the daughter of David and Sarah Semmes Floyd. She went on to become one of the most clever and resourceful operatives of the Civil War. When her younger brother, Bob, joined the Confederate army she and her mother remained on the Federal side of the Potomac. Their large, two-story brick home became a popular gathering place for Federal soldiers but the two women maintained close contact with their Confederate friends, and thus passed along Federal information as it became available. Many secrets were hidden in the hollow brass balls at the tops of the fireplace andirons, awaiting the arrival of a Confederate courier.[68]

In November 1862, Judge Advocate General L. C. Turner reported to Secretary of War Edwin M. Stanton that Olivia Floyd was known to be "engaged in all sorts of disloyal practices and in frequent and intimate communication" with Confederate agents. Turner then ordered her arrest and her transportation to the Old Capitol Prison in Washington. Sutprisingly, the order was never carried out and Miss Floyd continued her espionage activities until the very end of the war.

As the war came to a close, Olivia was an important link in a large chain of spies that operated between Richmond and Canada. The ring was instrumental in obtaining the release of fourteen Confederate officers who were about to be tried on criminal charges.[69] Messages and papers were forwarded to Olivia and promptly hidden in the andirons. When the Yankees came to search Rose Hill, they were invited to search the premises, which they did, and after the search was completed, they were encouraged to sit in front of the fire to warm their feet upon the very andirons that concealed the messages, but they were never found.

Additional messages arrived later that week for Olivia sewn in a courier's vest lining. These were added to the messages stored in the andirons, and on February 15, all of the documents were gathered at her home and carried to the courthouse by a special courier. These actions, in turn, saved the Confederate prisoners from possible execution.[70]

Olivia exhibited psychic powers and her interest in the occult was popular; she also believed in ghosts and the spirit world. Her home was said to be guarded by a huge dog ghost (which had been experienced by various people), and was noted by laymen as late as 1925. This rumor kept many

Yankees, as well as Confederates, from crossing Olivia's doorstep after midnight. [71]

One of the Confederate officers, Colonel Bennett Young, learned of Olivia's assistance in his liberation and invited her to be his guest at a reunion of Confederate veterans. To her surprise, Olivia was the honored guest. The reunion at Louisville was the high point of her declining years, and she returned to Rose Hill to talk of the event the rest of her life.

She died on a bright December day in 1905, and was buried in the parish cemetery beside her brother, Bob. It has been said that all of Charles County mourned because there would never be another person like Miss Olivia of Rose Hill. [72]

Carrie Lawton

Carrie Lawton moved to Richmond, Virginia, at the request of the Union Secret Service. She pretended to be a Southern lady who had been driven out of Maryland and she quickly made friends and was accepted in social circles. John Scobell, the first Negro operative, was assigned to serve as her assistant because he could easily be passed off as a servant. He was ordered to not leave Carrie alone when she was out of her residence, and was permitted to work independently as an operative only when she entertained houseguests.

The information gained by the two was forwarded by a separate courier to General George McClellan. As the situation grew more tense in Richmond, McClellan decided that he needed a line of direct communication in the Confederate capital. Hugh Lawton, Carrie's husband, was one of McClellan's officers, and the general decided to use the nightly rendezvous of the couple as an important link in his espionage network.

The couple met at an inn in Glendale operated by a Union sympathizer. Carrie, with Scobell as her groom, was easily granted passes to go riding in the afternoons; the sight of an attractive Southern belle, well-mounted, always raised the morale of the war-weary soldiers. The pair easily came and went as they pleased.

When Carrie and Hugh met at the inn, they would exchange riding crops, and thereby exchange messages and documents; the handles of the riding crops were hollowed out to conceal tissue paper messages. Scobell always served as a sentry during the Lawtons' meetings, thus making the transactions secure.

The inn was used not only by Federal operatives but also by Confederates. One evening, an overly friendly peddler came to the inn, frivolously spending his money. Carrie quickly realized that he was actually a Confederate counter-agent, but he disappeared after the evening meal, and the Lawtons were relieved. The relief soon turned to fear, however, because Carrie learned that the peddler left to organize his men in an attempt to capture her on the way back to Richmond.

After Hugh returned to his unit, Carrie decided she and Scobell would try to "ride" their way out of Glendale. Two swift mounts were prepared and Scobell packed a Smith and Wesson on his horse. The pair rode carefully through the night, avoiding the road when possible, but the full moon soon revealed the pair to the Rebel soldiers who were looking for them. Carrie was twenty miles from the safety of the Union line and they did their very best to outrun the Confederates. The Union steeds were spurred to a full gallop but they were simply no match for the fresh Confederate mounts. Consequently, they were soon overtaken.

At this point, Scobell's horse stepped in a gopher hole and broke its leg. Carrie started back for him but he waved her away. He waited until the Rebel soldiers were in range and fired six shots, killing two, wounding one, and scaring two others. This enabled Carrie's escape, and once safely behind Union lines, she located her husband and they set off to find Scobell. He was found safe, nursing the wounded Confederate.

This adventure ended Carrie Lawton's espionage experiences because it was not safe for her to continue. The Confederates wanted to execute her, and therefore, she was sent to safety behind the Union lines until the war was over.

Mrs. E.H. Baker

Originally a Richmond, Virginia, native, Mrs. E. H. Baker moved to Chicago when the Civil War began. In the fall of 1862 she was recruited by the Union Secret Service to operate between Richmond and Washington. In December 1862, she was assigned to gain the confidence of her old friends in Richmond in an attempt to gain entrance to the Tredegar Iron Works, in which the Confederate ironclad was being constructed. Security was extremely tight, and no male Federal agents were permitted to enter the Works.

Mrs. Baker found acceptance with Confederate Captain Atwater and his wife, and was welcomed into their Richmond home. They introduced her into the Richmond social circles and she quickly acquired many friends, always being careful to keep a neutral view of the war. Her social calendar kept her moving about Richmond, and she easily memorized and documented the city's fortifications.

Using extreme caution, she quietly and seductively hinted to Captain Atwater that she would like to see the Tredegar Iron Works. He complied to her request and secured her a pass and acted as her escort on a tour of the factory. While on the tour, she saw many experimental weapons, such as the new submarine battery (now called a water mine), a submarine ram (a rod on the bow of a ship tipped with a mine used to ram the enemy's vessel), and the prototype of the C.S.S. *Virginia* (also referred to as the Ironclad *Merrimac*). Later that day Mrs. Baker made sketches of the weapons and stitched them in her bonnet lining.

A few days later, using the excuse that war upset her too much to stay long in one place, Mrs. Baker asked Captain Atwater to secure her a pass so she could return to Chicago. The Atwaters sympathized with her and Captain Atwater obliged her request. She left Richmond and within twenty-four hours the weapon sketches were in the hands of Union authorities.

This is the only known escapade of Mrs. E. H. Baker, although she was a Federal operative between Washington and Richmond throughout the war. [73]

The Tredegar Iron Works, Richmond, Va.

The Confederate ironclad Merrimac *(C.S.S.* Virginia*).*

Little Known Operatives

There are many female operatives who are only briefly mentioned in the history of the Civil War. These ladies were often mentioned only upon their arrest, such as Ella (Ellie) M. Poole of Virginia. She was arrested in Wheeling, West Virginia, on October 6, 1861, because she sneaked documents that were hidden inside the lining of her guitar case into the city. She was housed for awhile in "Fort Greenhow," but escaped through the basement. At the time of her escape, she suffered from a severe attack of rheumatism, her body racked with pain and fever. She took refuge in a neighboring house, staying just ahead of the Yankees.

She, like Clara Judd, was taken captive by Delos Blythe, the relentless Federal detective in Vincennes, Indiana. She was never tried, however, but she was incarcerated in the Old Capitol Prison until her release in June, 1862.

Another agent was Jane Ferguson, a Tennessee teenager with an appearance that was "frank and simple as a child," who dressed as a Union soldier and crossed the Yankee lines to gain information for the Confederates. When captured by the Federals, she was sentenced to be hanged but the sentence was later reversed.

Mary and Sophia Overstreet of Tennessee were nineteen-year-old twin sisters who carried messages and documents for Captain John W. Headley (who later became Mary's husband). These girls would not have gotten into trouble with the Yankees had they not tried to save Sallie and Dollie Butler who had been mistakenly arrested by the Federals. The twins were arrested in May 1865, and released shortly thereafter.

Robbie Woodruff of Mississippi was a farm girl who walked ten miles to town to collect Confederate dispatches. Her extreme attractiveness did not hamper her activities, and she used it to overpower many Yankee soldiers who stopped her for a pass. It was her practice to drop the dispatches that she acquired into a designated hollow tree or stump where they would later be picked up. Interestingly, she was never captured by the Union.

Ann and Kate Patterson of Nashville assisted the Confederate cause by smuggling secrets, maps, and supplies in the false bottom of their father's doctor's buggy. They also used a lighted or darkened window to signal Confederates regarding the location of Federal troops. The Confederate sirens were instrumental in foiling many attempts of Federal "cattle buyers" who were actually Union spies.

Betty Haynes and Bettie Puckett of Triune, Tennessee, were couriers for DeWitt Smith Jobe, an operative member of Coleman's Confederate Scouts. They concealed and smuggled a great deal of information in the soles of their shoes.

Mary Dodge, Mary Swindle, and Minerva Cogburn of Little Rock, Arkansas, carried information and letters for David Dodd, the male spy for several Confederate officers. The women used hidden pockets in their clothing and false handles in their parasols to conceal their secret information.

Aurelia Burton assisted General Beauregard by carrying letters and documents in her camisole. She was caught in September 1862, and arrested, but she was eventually released.

Molly Tatum and Carrie Gray of Petersburg, Virginia, kept a steady flow of information to General George D. Shadburne, a personal operative for Robert E. Lee. The girls assumed the roles of loyalists, but were deadly Confederates. They once saved Shadburne from capture by hiding him in an upstairs bedroom while one of the maidens had a "hard fit." The Yankees who sought Shadburne did not search the house because they were unwilling to intrude upon a domestic crisis.

Sallie Pollock of Cumberland, Maryland, was not yet eighteen years of age when she was arrested on April 12, 1864, by Union agents. She was charged with carrying Confederate secrets down the Shenandoah Valley to Staunton, Virginia, in her vegetable basket. She served some time in the Old Capitol Prison but was eventually released.

The actions of these ladies, whether Confederate or Union, were above and beyond the call of duty. All deserved the homage of a grateful nation, regardless of the side they served. They took unnecessary risks, forcing their way into situations that their masculine counterparts could not (or perhaps would not) enter, and proved themselves as outstanding people to their allies.

The Civil War did not witness the execution of any female operatives (but two or three were imprisoned with a death sentence), and it was chiefly masculine chivalry that prevailed and allowed their lives to be spared. Regardless, from any standard, these ladies of espionage served in the way they knew best, without acknowledging threats to life or reputation. They truly are *Blue and Gray Roses of Intrigue.*

End Notes

[1] Diaries of Mary Greenhow Lee, daughter of Rose Greenhow (1891).

[2] Mrs. Rose Greenhow's seized correspondence housed in the National Archives, Washington, DC.

[3] Captain Joseph Hazelton, *Scouts, Spies, and Heroes* (Cincinnati, 1892), p. 79.

[4] *Ibid.*, p. 92.

[5] From the collection of Rose Greenhow's letters housed at DukeUniversity.

[6] *Ibid.*

[7] Colonel L.E. Marie, Jr. (Rose Greenhow's grandson), *Memoirs of Rose*, 1901.

[8] Rose Greenhow, *My Imprisonment and the First Year of Abolition Rule in Washington* (London, August 1863), p. 59.

[9] *Confederate States of America Despatch Book*, 102, vol. 6, p. 336.

[10] Lomax, Virginia, *The Old Capitol and Its Inmate* (New York, 1867), p. 26.

[11] Greenhow. *My Imprisonment*, p. 79.

[12] *Ibid.*, p. 86.

[13] J. E. Cooke, *Wearing of the Gray* (New York, 1893), pp. 418-423.

[14] Harry Hayden's account of Mrs. Greenhow's death (lodged in New Hanover, North Carolina's Historical Commision).

[15] "Antonio," *Southern Observer* (Sewanee, Virginia, 1873).

[16] *Ibid.*

[17] Cooke, 102.

[18] Charles W. Russell, editor, *Memoirs of Colonel John Mosby* (Boston, 1917), p. 21.

[19] Lafayette Baker, *History of U.S. Secret Service* (Philadelphia, 1867), p. 480.

[20] *Ibid.*, p. 495.

[21] Belle Boyd, *Belle Boyd Starts Her Work as a Spy* (Cincinnati, 1867), p. 400.

[22] Diary of Mrs. Rowland (Belle Boyd's sister), housed in the historical archives of the State of Virginia.

[23] Boyd, p .425.

[24] General Jackson's report on operations in the valley, May 14-June 17, 1862.

[25] *Ibid.*

[26] Lomax, p. 36.

[27] *New York Dramatic Mirror*, November 20, 1897.

[28] Mrs. A. Michael (Belle Boyd's daughter), *Memoirs of Belle* (New York, 1893), p. 462.

[29] Baker-Union papers (National Archives, Washington, DC, 1861-1864).

[30] Van Lew Manuscript Collection, New York Public Library.

[31] *Ibid.*

[32] *Ibid.*

[33] *Ibid.*

[34] Madeline Dahlgren, *Memoirs of John A. Dahlgren* (Boston, 1882), p. 96.

[35] Van Lew Manuscript Collection.

[36] Hazelton, p. 101.

[37] Van Lew Manuscript Collection.

[38] Official Records of Union and Confederate Armies, 1860-1901 (Washington, DC), Series 2, Vol. 8, p. 992.

[39] Sarah Emma Edmonds, *Nurse and Spy* (Hartford, CT, 1864), p. 59.

[40] Sarah Emma Edmonds, *A Female Spy Changes Her Colors* (Hartford, CT, 1867), p. 63.

[41] P.L. Sarmiento, *Life of Pauline Cushman* (Phildelphia, 1866), p. 36.

[42] Baker. *History*, p. 512.

[43] Sarmiento, p. 86.

[44] "The Case of Miss Carroll," *Century Magazine*, August 1890.

[45] Sarah E. Blackwell, *A Military Genius, The Life of Anna Ella Carroll* (Washington, DC, 1891-1895), 2 volumes.

[46] Anna Ella Carroll, *The Tennessee Plan* (handwritten document, Maryland Historical Society, Baltimore, November 30, 1861).

[47] Baker. History, p. 617.

[48] Russell, p. 46.

[49] *Ibid.*, p. 93.

[50] Hazelton, p. 216.

[51] Davis Burke, *Civil War: Strange and Fascinating Facts* (New York, 1982), p. 115.

[52] Bell Irvin Wiley, *Confederate Women* (Westport, CT, 1960), p. 9.

[53] *Ibid.*, p. 27.

[54] Bell Irvin Wiley, *Embattled Confederates* (New York, 1964). p. 164.

[55] *Ibid.*, p. 166.

[56] *Ibid.*, p. 170.

[57] Hamilton Cochran, *Blockade Runners of the Confederacy* (Indianapolis, 1958), pp. 131-154.

[58] Burke. *Confederate Women*, p. 56.

[59] C.J. Worthington, editor, *Woman in Battle, A Narrative of the Exploits, Adventures, and Travels of Loreta Janita Velazquez* (Hartford, CT, 1874).

[60] Bell. *Embattled Confederates*, p. 183.

[61] Greenhow. *My Imprisonment*, p. 73.

[62] Captured correspondence of the Dix-Pierrepont Commission, National Archives, Washington, DC, 1862-1863.

[63] Cooke, p. 210.

[64] Phillip Parton, *General Butler in New Orleans* (New York, 1864), p. 31.

[65] *Ibid.*, p. 37.

[66] Mary E. Massey, *Bonnet Brigades* (New York, 1867), p. 10.

[67] *Ibid.*, p. 26.

[68] "Echoes of the Past," *Maryland Post*, May, 1908.

[69] *Ibid.*

[70] *Ibid.*

[71] *Ibid.*

[72] Baker-Union Papers.

[73] John Bakeless, *Spies for the Confederacy* (Philadelphia, 1975) pp. 89-125.

Selected Reading List

_____. "Antonio." *Southern Observer*. Sewanee, VA, August 1873.

Bakeless, John. *Spies for the Confederacy*. Philadelphia, 1970.

Baker, Lafayette. *History of U.S. Secret Service*. Philadelphia, 1867.

Baker-Union Papers. National Archives. Washington, DC, 1861-1864.

Blackwell, Sarah E. *A Military Genius, Life of Anna Ella Carroll*. Washington, DC, 1891-1895.

Botkin, B.A. *Civil War Treasury of Tales, Legends, and Folklore*. New York, 1899.

Boyd, Belle. *Belle Boyd in Camp and Prison*. New York, 1899.

_ _ _. *Belle Boyd Starts Her Work as a Spy*. Cincinnati, 1867.

Burke, Davis. *Civil War: Strange and Fascinating Facts*. New York, 1982.

Carroll, Anna Ella. *Great American Battle*. New York, 1856.

_ _ _. *The Tennessee Plan*, a handwritten document. Maryland Historical Society. Baltimore, November 30, 1861.

_____. "The Case of Miss Carroll." *Century Magazine*. August 1890.

Cochran, Hamilton. *Blockade Runners of the Confederacy*. Indianapolis, 1958.

Confederate States of America Despatch Book.

Cooke, John Esten (staff member of General J.E.B. Stuart). *Wearing of the Gray*. Bloomington, IN, 1893.

Dahlgren, Madeline. *Memoirs of John A. Dahlgren*. Boston, 1882.

Dix-Pierrepont Commission Correspondence (captured by the C.S.A.) 1861-1865.

Eaton, Clement. *History of Southern Confederacy*. New York, 1954.

_____. "Echoes From the Past." *Maryland Post*, 1908.

Edmonds, Sarah Emma. *A Female Spy Changes Her Colors*. Hartford, CT, 1867.

_ _ _. *Nurse and Spy*. Hartford, CT, 1864.

Fostes, G. Allen. *The Eyes and Ears of the Civil War*. New York, 1963.

Gilmer, Harry (commander of the Second Maryland Battalion). *Four Years in the Saddle*. New York, 1866.

Greenhow, Rose. Letter collection, housed at Duke University.

_ _ _. *My Imprisonment and the First Year of Abolition Rule*. Washington, D.C., August 1863.

_ _ _. Seized correspondence, housed in the National Archives in Washington, DC.

Hossler, William W. *General and His Lady*. Chapel Hill, NC, 1965.

Hayden, Harry. Account of Rose Greenhow's death, housed in New Hanover, NC Historical Commission, 1966.

Hazelton, Joseph, Captain, (C.S.A.). *Scouts, Spies, and Heroes*. Cincinnati, 1892.

Hergerheimer, Joseph. *Swords and Roses*. New York, 1928.

Howell, Richard. *Confederate Reader*. New York, 1957.

Ind, Allison, Colonel. *A Short History of Espionage*. New York, 1963.

General Jackson's report on operations in the valley. May 14-June 17, 1862.

Kane, Edward T. *Spies for the Blue and Gray*. New York, 1954.

Ketchum, Richard M., editor. *Picture History of the Civil War*. New York, 1960.

Knight, Ruth Adams. *Woman with a Sword*. New York, 1948.

Komoroff, Manual. *True Adventures of Spies*. Boston, 1954.

Lee, Mary Greenhow. Diaries (Rose Greenhow's daughter), 1891.

Lomax, Virginia. *The Old Capitol and Its Inmates*. New York, 1867.

Marie, L.E., Jr., Colonel (Rose Greenhow's grandson). Memoirs of Rose, 1901.

Massey, Mary Elizabeth. *Bonnet Brigades*. New York, 1967.

_____. *Refugee Life in the Confederacy*. Baton Rouge, LA, 1964.

McPherson, James M. *Ordeal by Fire*. New York, 1982.

Michael, Mrs. A. Diaries (Belle Boyd's daughter). Memoirs of Belle.

New York Dramatic Mirror. November 20, 1897.

Official Records of Union and Confederate Armies 1860-1901, Washington, D.C.

Parish, Peter J. *American Civil War*. New York, 1975.

Parton, Phelps. *General Butler in New Orleans*. New York, 1864.

Pinkerton, Allan. *The Founder of the Pinkerton Shadows A Beautiful Rebel Spy*. Washington, 1880.

_ _ _. *Spy of the Rebellion*. New York, 1883.

Ross, Ishbell. *Rebel Rose*. Simon Island, GA, 1954.

Rowland, Mrs. Diary (Belle Boyd's sister), housed in the historical archives of the state of Virginia.

Russell, Charles W., editor. *Memoirs of Colonel John S. Mosby*. Boston, 1917.

_ _ _. *Mosby's War Reminiscences*. New York, 1887.

Sarmiento, P.L. *The Life of Pauline Cushman*. Philadelphia, 1866.

Sikafis, Stewart. *Who Was Who in the Civil War*. New York, 1988.

Sigaud, Louis A. *Belle Boyd, Confederate Spy*. Richmond, 1944.

Singer, Jurt and Jane Sherrod. *Spies for the Democracy*. Minneapolis, 1960.

Van Dorn Stern, Philip. *Secret Missions of the Civil War*. New York, 1959.

Van Lew Manuscript Collection, New York Public Library.

Wilder, Arthur. *Adventures in Black*. New York, 1962.

Wiley, Bell Irvin. *Confederate Women*. Westport, CT, 1960.

_ _ _. *Embattled Confederates*. New York, 1964.

Wise, Winfred E. *Mr. Lincoln's Secret Weapon*. Philadelphia, 1961.

Worthington, C.J., editor. *Woman in Battle, A Narrative of the Exploits, Adventures, and Travels of Loreta Janita Velazquez*. Hartford, CT, 1874.

Photo Credits

From *On Hazardous Service*, by William Gilmore Beymer, 26

From *My Dear Lady*, by Marjorie Barstow Greenbie, 35

Library of Congress, 9

Lloyd Ostendorf Collection, Dayton, OH, 32

From *The Spy of the Rebellion*, by Allan Pinkerton, 36

United States Army Military History Institute, 11, 14 (2), 22 (bottom), 23 (2), 25, 30, 38, 42, 47 (2), 52, 55 (2), 62 (2)

Valentine Museum, Richmond, 22 (top)

William L. Clements Library, The University of Michigan, 19

THOMAS PUBLICATIONS publishes books about the American Colonial era, the Revolutionary War, the Civil War, and other important topics. For a complete list of titles, please write to:

THOMAS PUBLICATIONS
P. O. Box 3031
Gettysburg, PA 17325